INTRODUCTION

THE INTUITIVE
WARDROBE CLEANSE
FORMULA

YOUR STYLE
ALIGNED
SERIES

By 'Chandra-Lucinda' the founder of 'Intuitive Style'

CONTENTS

01 - 05
INTRODUCTION

MODULE 1: 06-25
WARDROBE ORGANISATION

MODULE 2: 26-35
WARDROBE THEMES

MODULE 3: 36-51
WARDROBE CLEANSE METHODS

MODULE 4: 52-73
COMMENCING A WARDROBE RESET DETOX

MODULE 5: 74-105
NEW STYLE COMBINATIONS

106-107
CONGRATULATIONS! YOUR WARDROBE CLEANSE IS COMPLETE

108-147
STYLE NOTEBOOK

INTRODUCTION

When you feel cluttered in
your wardrobe, you may feel
cluttered in your mind.

INTRODUCTION

A clear and organised wardrobe can help you express your unique style easily.

INTRODUCTION

THE BENEFITS OF A WARDROBE CLEANSE

Developing a healthy relationship with our wardrobes and clothing pieces is essential to help keep our unique styles flowing.

This guide encourages us to let go of what is no longer serving us in our wardrobes, creating space for our authentic styles to bloom.

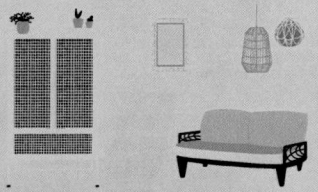

MODULE 1

WARDROBE ORGANISATION

FOUNDATIONAL STYLE TIPS THAT WILL HELP
POSITIVE ENERGY FLOW IN YOUR WARDROBE

Organise Your Wardrobe With Your Favourite Tips,
And Complete The Q&A Workbook

WARDROBE ORGANISATION

MODULE 1

1. INVEST IN QUALITY OVER QUANTITY

Invest in pieces that last, especially the wardrobe basics.

2. SHOP MINDFULLY

Shop for complimentary clothing pieces that support your values, body type and style vision.

WARDROBE ORGANISATION

MODULE 1

3. USE MATCHING HANGERS

The right hanger will support your garment, making your wardrobe look tidy and organised.

4. HANG SIMILAR ITEMS TOGETHER

It's far simpler to bring an outfit together when we can easily see the clothing pieces in our wardrobes.

WARDROBE ORGANISATION

MODULE 1

5. COLD WASH CYCLE

Opting for a cold wash cycle or hand washing your apparel can extend the life cycle of your clothing. Always check your label first.

6. STORAGE

Out-of-season clothing pieces or sentimental Items you're no longer wearing, opt for storing them away in a storage container.

WARDROBE ORGANISATION

MODULE 1

7.
USE GARMENT CARE INSTRUCTIONS

Follow the care advice on your garment to increase the item's longevity.

8.
FOOTWEAR

Use shelving to keep your footwear off the floor, or store them in clear boxes that are easily accessible.

WARDROBE ORGANISATION

MODULE 1

9.
A FUNCTIONAL SPACE

Use the front of your wardrobe and easily accessible zones for most worn items. Store your least-worn pieces, such as evening wear, in the quiet zones of your wardrobe.

10.
DRAW DIVIDERS

Use draw dividers or small boxes to divide small items like socks, underwear, hosiery, nightwear, and bras.

WARDROBE ORGANISATION

MODULE 1

11.
SMALL BOXES
Small boxes are perfect for storing belts, underwear & socks.

12.
ALTER CLOTHING
Alter your clothing to fit your body type. You will get more wear when your clothing pieces complement your unique shape.

WARDROBE ORGANISATION

MODULE 1

13.
ACCESSORIES
Create an area especially for your accessories, such as jewellery, scarves, and hats.

14.
SHELVING
Use the shelving in your wardrobe for knitwear or heavier clothing items.

WARDROBE ORGANISATION

MODULE 1

15.
MULTIPLE ITEM HANGER

These hangers are perfect for bringing similar clothing pieces together or grouping an outfit.

16.
SMALLER WARDROBES

Create extra room by using a clothes rack, installing a wall shelf or using a small bookshelf that will fit inside your wardrobe.

WARDROBE ORGANISATION

MODULE 1

**17.
EDIT YOUR WARDROBE**
Keep editing your wardrobe over time. Be open to growing with your unique style and experimenting with new outfit combinations.

**18.
ONE IN ONE OUT**
Let go of one clothing piece when another is ready to enter your wardrobe.
It will help reduce wardrobe clutter.

WARDROBE ORGANISATION

MODULE 1

19.
ORGANISE BY WARDROBE THEMES

Creating a wardrobe theme will help everything look organised and tidy.
Plus, it can save you time getting ready.

20.
WEAR COLOURS THAT COMPLIMENT YOU

Wearing colours that work with your unique colour palette will help you feel radiant and at your best.

WARDROBE ORGANISATION

MODULE 1

21. QUALITY STAPLES

Invest in quality staple pieces that allow you to mix and match outfits effortlessly, feel timeless, and can last for years to come.

22. SPEND LESS ON FASHION TRENDS

Trends come and go quickly. Adding a couple of inexpensive on-trend pieces will help you feel fresh and updated.

WARDROBE ORGANISATION

MODULE 1

YOUR WARDROBE SPACE

HAVE A PEEK AT YOUR WARDROBE AND NOTE THE FIRST THREE THINGS THAT COME TO MIND.

1. _____
   _____
   _____

2. _____
   _____
   _____

3. _____
   _____
   _____

WARDROBE ORGANISATION

MODULE 1

HOW CAN YOU USE YOUR WARDROBE SPACE MORE EFFICIENTLY?

_____
_____
_____
_____

WHICH WARDROBE ORGANISATION TIPS WOULD YOU LIKE TO USE IN YOUR CLOSET?

_____
_____
_____
_____
_____
_____
_____
_____

WARDROBE ORGANISATION

MODULE 1

USE THIS SPACE TO NOTE YOUR
WARDROBE ORGANISATION TIPS

WARDROBE ORGANISATION

MODULE 1

USE THIS SPACE TO NOTE YOUR
WARDROBE ORGANISATION TIPS

WARDROBE ORGANISATION

MODULE 1

USE THIS SPACE TO NOTE YOUR
WARDROBE ORGANISATION TIPS

WARDROBE ORGANISATION

MODULE 1

RECAP TIME: WHAT HAVE YOU LEARNED IN THIS MODULE?

WARDROBE ORGANISATION

MODULE 1

In this module, you have gained valuable insights and ideas to organise your wardrobe effectively.

You can now select and implement the methods that best suit the needs of your wardrobe, making it more functional and easy to manage.

MODULE 2

WARDROBE THEMES

A WARDROBE THEME HELPS YOU EXPRESS YOUR UNIQUE STYLE WITH EASE

Review The Different Types Of Wardrobe Themes and Fill Out the Q&A Workbook.

WARDROBE THEMES

MODULE 2

WARDROBE THEME 1

BY ASPECTS OF YOUR LIFE

Create five categories that work with your lifestyle and wardrobe needs.

> EXAMPLE:
> 30% Everyday wear
> 30% Professional wear
> 15% Social wear
> 15% Relaxed days wear
> %10 Activewear

Assess if your wardrobe matches your lifestyle or if anything is out of balance.

See where you can realign your wardrobe to match your lifestyle better.

WARDROBE THEMES

MODULE 2

WARDROBE THEME 2
SEASONAL WEAR

- Summer
- Spring
- Autumn
- Winter

Store away your off-season clothing in a box with a lid.

Create a capsule wardrobe with complementary seasonal colours and clothing pieces.

Then organise your wardrobe by colour/ weight.

WARDROBE THEMES

MODULE 2

WARDROBE THEME 3

BY CATEGORIES/STYLES

- Jumpers
- Dresses
- Skirts
- Pants/Jeans
- Tops
- Blazers/Jackets

Organise your categories/styles by section and then by colour/weight

WARDROBE THEMES

MODULE 2

WARDROBE THEME 4

BY OUTFIT

Pre-select your outfit combinations for the week ahead using multi-layer hangers.

For example use
one multi-layer hanger
with five or fewer items.

- High waisted Pants
- Cropped Tee
- Oversized Blazer
- Accessories

When organising your wardrobe by outfit, it is recommended to pre-plan at least 5-7 outfits.

These outfits could be for the upcoming week, casual days, or special events.

Any items that are not being selected for pre-planned outfits should be stored in a non-primary zone of your closet, categorised by colour and style for easy access.

WARDROBE THEMES

MODULE 2

WARDROBE THEME 5

CREATE A WARDROBE THEME OF YOUR OWN

NOTE YOUR IDEAS BELOW.

_____

_____

_____

_____

_____

_____

Further examples are grouping by colours and length of your apparel or combining two themes like seasonal and aspects of your life.

WARDROBE THEMES

MODULE 2

NOTE YOUR CHOSEN WARDROBE THEME AND WHY YOU FEEL IT WORKS WITH YOUR SPACE AND UNIQUE STYLE.

_____

_____

_____

_____

_____

_____

_____

_____

_____

WARDROBE THEMES

MODULE 2

NOTE FOUR CHANGES YOU WOULD LIKE TO EMBRACE FROM TODAY TOWARDS MAKING YOUR WARDROBE FUNCTIONAL.

1. _____
   _____

2. _____
   _____

3. _____
   _____

4. _____
   _____

WARDROBE THEMES

MODULE 2

RECAP TIME: WHAT HAVE YOU LEARNED IN THIS MODULE?

WARDROBE THEMES

MODULE 2

In this module, you have been introduced to the concept of a wardrobe theme and learned how it can be an effective tool for maintaining a functional wardrobe.

By having a clear vision for your wardrobe, you can more easily organise and declutter your clothing collection, making it easier to find and wear outfits that make you feel confident and comfortable.

MODULE 3

WARDROBE CLEANSE METHODS

WARDROBE CLEANSE-METHODS THAT KEEP YOUR UNIQUE STYLE FLOWING

Read Through The Wardrobe Cleanse Methods And Choose One To Two Detox Strategies.

WARDROBE CLEANSE METHODS

MODULE 3

WARDROBE CLEANSE METHOD 1

A PERIODIC WARDROBE DETOX

Consider scheduling a periodic wardrobe detox to maintain a well-organised and uncluttered wardrobe.

You can do this every two weeks or once a month, whichever works best for you.

This simple practice will keep your closet in tip-top shape and make getting ready in the morning a breeze.

WARDROBE CLEANSE METHODS

MODULE 3

FORTNIGHTLY WARDROBE DETOX

Transform how you approach your wardrobe by dedicating 10-20 minutes every couple of weeks to refresh and detox your wardrobe.

Here are some quick tips to help you:

1. Schedule 10-20 minutes every couple of weeks to review and refresh your wardrobe.

2. Remove any clutter that might be occupying space in your wardrobe and create more breathing space.

3. Categorise similar items such as tops, pants, and dresses. You can also group them by colour for easy access.

By following these tips, you'll be amazed at how it can transform your daily getting-ready routine.

WARDROBE CLEANSE METHODS

MODULE 3

MONTHLY WARDROBE DETOX

Take the time every month to declutter your wardrobe and align yourself with your wardrobe theme.

Here are some quick tips to detox your wardrobe monthly:

1. Schedule 30-45 minutes in your calendar each month to declutter your wardrobe.

2. Remove all your clothes from your wardrobe and let the natural air cleanse your items.

3. Experiment with different clothing combinations and ask yourself if there are any changes you'd like to make to improve your style.

4. Make sure to align any items out of place in your closet with your chosen wardrobe theme.

Following these tips, you can ensure you always look and feel your best.

WARDROBE CLEANSE METHODS

MODULE 3

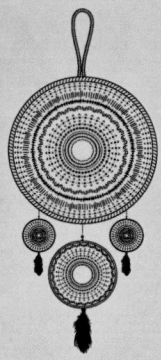

WARDROBE CLEANSE METHOD 2

A SEASONAL WARDROBE DETOX

> Refresh your wardrobe and mindset with the changing seasons.
>
> With a fresh wardrobe and a fresh mindset, you'll be ready to take on whatever the new season brings.

WARDROBE CLEANSE METHODS

MODULE 3

SEASONAL WARDROBE DETOX

Cleanse your wardrobe every three months and work with the elements of nature.

Here are some quick tips to detox your wardrobe seasonally:

1. Spend a couple of hours mixing and matching your seasonal wardrobe and organising and cleaning your space.

2. Use storage boxes with lids to store away clothing items that are out of season. Please make sure to keep the containers in a cool, dry place.

3. If you're cleaning out your wardrobe in the warmer seasons, open your windows to let in fresh air and sunshine.

In the cooler seasons, pick a day when the weather is dry and sunny to air out your wardrobe—helping circulate the air and dry out any moisture.

4. Use natural deodorisers: Place natural deodorisers like lavender sachets or activated charcoal to keep your wardrobe smelling fresh. Cedar blocks are also helpful for cleansing your space and protecting your clothes from insects and moths.

5. Set a reminder to align your wardrobe and energy with the changing seasons.

As the seasons change, view it as an opportunity to realign your wardrobe with your unique style.

WARDROBE CLEANSE METHODS

MODULE 3

WARDROBE CLEANSE METHOD 3

A RESET WARDROBE DETOX

> Revamping your wardrobe every six months or annually is a great way to keep it up-to-date, fresh, and organised.
>
> It's a chance to update your style and wardrobe, consider more sustainable options, and feel confident in your style choices.

WARDROBE CLEANSE METHODS

MODULE 3

METHOD 3

EVERY SIX MONTHS OR YEARLY, GIVE YOUR CLOSET A RESET WARDROBE DETOX.

Our wardrobe rest detox guide takes you step-by-step through the process from start to finish.

Please take a look at pages 52-73 for your guide.

WARDROBE CLEANSE METHODS

MODULE 3

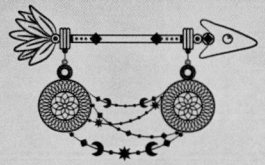

WARDROBE CLEANSE METHOD 4

AN ENERGETIC WARDROBE CLEANSE

Imagine feeling a deeper connection to your unique style, and experiencing a sense of joy and positivity as you select your outfits each day.

By cleansing your wardrobe with high-vibe energy, you can awaken your spiritual and creative essence, and enhance your overall well-being.

Whether you choose to let the natural air purify your clothes or incorporate crystals into your space, these methods can help you embrace your unique style with confidence and enthusiasm.

WARDROBE CLEANSE METHODS

MODULE 3

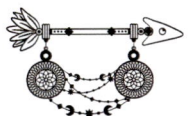

#1 DETOX YOUR CLOTHING IN SALTWATER OR USE NATURAL SOAPS/DETERGENTS, THEN HANG TO DRY IN THE SUNLIGHT.

Put some salt in a bucket. Leave your items to soak for a little while. Then wash as usual.

Additionally, you can place a bowl of salt in the corner of your wardrobe to absorb any unwanted energies. Remember to remove the salt after a couple of days.

Please make sure to read the care instructions for your item carefully. It's important to double-check beforehand that your fabrics won't be damaged by exposure to salt or sunlight.

WARDROBE CLEANSE METHODS

MODULE 3

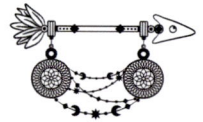

#2 HANGING YOUR CLOTHES IN SUNLIGHT OR FRESH AIR.

Sunlight or fresh air is another powerful method of detoxing energy from your clothing.

METHOD:
Leave them stretched out or on a hanger for 12 to 24 hours. Allow the fresh air to purify your clothing.

WARDROBE CLEANSE METHODS

MODULE 3

#3

SHIFT OR
DIFFUSE ENERGY
IN YOUR
WARDROBE WITH
CRYSTALS.

Recharge your favourite crystals in the moonlight or sunlight for twenty-four or forty-eight hours.

Place your charged crystals in a little pouch in your wardrobe; alternatively, line your crystals in the corners of your wardrobe.

Cleanse the energy of your crystals once a month and place them back in your wardrobe to boost the energy.

WARDROBE CLEANSE METHODS

MODULE 3

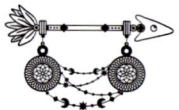

#4 PLAY HIGH-FREQUENCY ENERGY MUSIC FOR THIRTY MINUTES IN THE ROOM, WITH YOUR CLOSET.

Clear the energy of your wardrobe with high-frequency sound.

Search for sound frequencies such as 528Hz, 777Hz and 963Hz or cleanse the energy with a singing bowl.

WARDROBE CLEANSE METHODS

MODULE 3

CHOOSE YOUR FAVOURITE WARDROBE CLEANSE METHODS

1.

2.

3.

WARDROBE CLEANSE METHODS

MODULE 3

REVIEWING THE MODULE: WHAT HAVE YOU LEARNED?

_____
_____
_____
_____
_____
_____
_____
_____
_____
_____
_____
_____
_____
_____
_____

WARDROBE CLEANSE METHODS

MODULE 3

In this module, you've learned about different methods to cleanse your wardrobe and how they can positively impact your mood and self-confidence.

MODULE 4

WARDROBE RESET DETOX

REVIVE AND REFRESH YOUR CLOSET
WITH A WARDROBE RESET DETOX

Achieve a Complete Wardrobe Reset Detox with Our
Step-by-Step Guide.

WARDROBE CLEANSE RITUAL

MODULE 4

WARDROBE RESET DETOX

To begin your wardrobe cleanse ritual, set aside a few hours in your day and create a calm atmosphere with your favourite music and scents, such as candles or incense.

Allowing you to feel relaxed and centred as you begin letting go of clothing that no longer serves you.

If you need more guidance, take a look at the wardrobe detox questions for further assistance.

WARDROBE CLEANSE RITUAL

MODULE 4

WARDROBE DETOX QUESTIONS

HELPFUL QUESTIONS TO ASK YOURSELF WHEN DETOXING YOUR WARDROBE

1: Have you worn the clothing piece sometime in the previous 12 months?

2: Does it mix and match effortlessly with other items in your wardrobe?

3: Does this clothing piece represent your current style?

4: Do you feel comfortable wearing this item?

5: Is the item in good condition?

6: Does the item fit your body right now?

7: Does this item have sentimental value?

8: Do you feel happy wearing the clothing piece?

If you answer "no" to any of the questions above, it might be time to let go of the clothing item.

If you are unsure about whether to keep the item, store it away and see if you miss it.

If you find yourself missing the item, you can consider re-introducing it to your closet during your next wardrobe cleanse.

WARDROBE CLEANSE RITUAL

MODULE 4

STEP 1:
FIRST, SORT YOUR CLOTHES INTO THREE PILES: KEEP, MAYBE, AND ITEMS YOU NO LONGER WEAR. THIS INCLUDES SHOES, BAGS, AND ACCESSORIES.

PILE 1:
(KEEP PILE)

PILE 2:
(MAYBE PILE)

PILE 3:
(ITEMS THAT YOU NO LONGER WEAR PILE)

PLEASE TICK THE BOX PROVIDED AFTER PLACING EACH CLOTHING ITEM IN THE CORRECT PILE.

STEP 2:
YOU CAN ALLOCATE SIX BAGS OR SACKS FOR GIFTS, SALES, RECYCLING, DISPOSAL, CLOTHING REPAIRS, AND CLOTHES SWAPPING.

WARDROBE CLEANSE RITUAL

MODULE 4

PILE 1: KEEP PILE

STEP 2: ONCE YOUR CLOTHING PIECES ARE IN THE APPROPRIATE PILES.

PUT AWAY ANY ITEMS IN YOUR KEEP USING YOUR CHOSEN WARDROBE THEME.

Please double-check that your items in this pile are in good condition; they complement your body type and represent your current style.

WHEN COMPLETED TICK HERE

WARDROBE CLEANSE RITUAL

MODULE 4

PILE 2: MAYBE PILE

STEP 3: ASK YOURSELF IF YOU CAN SEE THE POTENTIAL FOR BRINGING ANY ITEMS FROM YOUR MAYBE PILE BACK INTO YOUR WARDROBE.

Using the wardrobe detox questions worksheet to help you move through the process.

WHEN COMPLETED TICK HERE ☐

WARDROBE CLEANSE RITUAL

MODULE 4

PILE 2: MAYBE PILE

☐ PLACE ANY ITEMS YOU WANT TO KEEP BACK IN YOUR WARDROBE USING YOUR WARDROBE THEME.

☐ ANY CLOTHING ITEMS THAT DO NOT MEET YOUR WARDROBE NEEDS YET ARE GOOD ENOUGH TO BE SOLD, GIFTED OR DONATED ARE TO BE PLACED IN THE APPROPRIATE BAGS/SACKS.

☐ PLACE ANY ITEMS YOU WANT REPAIR OR DISCARD/RECYCLE IN SEPARATE BAGS/SACKS.

WARDROBE CLEANSE RITUAL

MODULE 4

PILE 3: ITEMS THAT YOU NO LONGER WEAR

- [ ] PLACE ANY ITEMS YOU WANT TO KEEP BACK IN YOUR WARDROBE USING YOUR WARDROBE THEME.

- [ ] PLACE ITEMS TO BE SOLD, GIFTED, OR DONATED INTO THE APPROPRIATE BAGS/SACKS.

- [ ] PLACE ANY ITEMS YOU WANT TO REPAIR OR DISCARD /RECYCLE IN SEPARATE BIN BAGS/SACKS.

- [ ] YOU CAN PLACE SENTIMENTAL ITEMS IN A STORAGE CONTAINER OR SENTIMENTAL BOX FOR SAFEKEEPING.

WARDROBE CLEANSE RITUAL

MODULE 4

MAKE TIME TO COMPLETE THE
PROCESS FOR ITEMS IN BAGS/SACKS

- [ ] GIFT/CHARITY SHOP BAG
- [ ] SELL BAG
- [ ] RECYCLING BAG
- [ ] DISCARD BAG
- [ ] REPAIR BAG
- [ ] CLOTHES SWAP NIGHT

TICK THE BOXES ABOVE WHEN
YOU HAVE COMPLETED THE PROCESS

WARDROBE CLEANSE RITUAL

MODULE 4

NOW THAT YOU HAVE FINISHED THE CLEANSING PROCESS, PLEASE MAKE NOTE OF ANY GAPS IN YOUR WARDROBE THAT PREVENT AN OUTFIT FROM FEELING COMPLETE.

- [ ] _____
- [ ] _____
- [ ] _____
- [ ] _____
- [ ] _____
- [ ] _____
- [ ] _____
- [ ] _____

WARDROBE CLEANSE RITUAL

MODULE 4

CONSIDER CREATING A WARDROBE WISHLIST AND BUDGET FOR FUTURE PURCHASES.

- [ ] _____
- [ ] _____
- [ ] _____
- [ ] _____
- [ ] _____
- [ ] _____
- [ ] _____

BUDGET:

WARDROBE CLEANSE RITUAL

MODULE 4

To ensure that you stay on track with your wardrobe cleansing, schedule reminders in your calendar for your next two sessions.

Additionally, consider hosting a clothes swap night with your loved ones as an alternative way to refresh your wardrobe.

DATE: _____

WARDROBE
CLEANSE METHOD: _____

DATE: _____

WARDROBE
CLEANSE METHOD: _____

DATE: _____

CLOTHES
SWAP NIGHT: _____

With the following pages of this module, you will find space to record your wardrobe inventory.

This process can help you keep track of your items and maintain a consistent wardrobe colour scheme.

WARDROBE CLEANSE RITUAL

MODULE 4

KEEP TRACK OF YOUR ITEMS IN YOUR WARDROBE WITH
YOUR CURATED INVENTORY LISTS

WARDROBE INVENTORY
TOPS

- [ ] _____
- [ ] _____
- [ ] _____
- [ ] _____
- [ ] _____
- [ ] _____
- [ ] _____
- [ ] _____
- [ ] _____
- [ ] _____

WARDROBE CLEANSE RITUAL

MODULE 4

WARDROBE INVENTORY
BOTTOMS

- [ ]
- [ ]
- [ ]
- [ ]
- [ ]
- [ ]
- [ ]
- [ ]
- [ ]
- [ ]
- [ ]

WARDROBE CLEANSE RITUAL

MODULE 4

WARDROBE INVENTORY

SHOES

- [ ] _____
- [ ] _____
- [ ] _____
- [ ] _____
- [ ] _____
- [ ] _____
- [ ] _____
- [ ] _____
- [ ] _____
- [ ] _____
- [ ] _____
- [ ] _____

WARDROBE CLEANSE RITUAL

MODULE 4

WARDROBE INVENTORY
ACCESSORIES

- [ ]
- [ ]
- [ ]
- [ ]
- [ ]
- [ ]
- [ ]
- [ ]
- [ ]
- [ ]
- [ ]

WARDROBE CLEANSE RITUAL

MODULE 4

WARDROBE INVENTORY
LAYERS

- [ ] _____
- [ ] _____
- [ ] _____
- [ ] _____
- [ ] _____
- [ ] _____
- [ ] _____
- [ ] _____
- [ ] _____
- [ ] _____
- [ ] _____
- [ ] _____

WARDROBE CLEANSE RITUAL

MODULE 4

WARDROBE INVENTORY
OTHERS

- [ ] _____
- [ ] _____
- [ ] _____
- [ ] _____
- [ ] _____
- [ ] _____
- [ ] _____
- [ ] _____
- [ ] _____
- [ ] _____
- [ ] _____
- [ ] _____

WARDROBE CLEANSE RITUAL

MODULE 4

TO MAINTAIN A COHESIVE COLOUR PALETTE IN YOUR WARDROBE, USE THIS SPACE TO IDENTIFY YOUR PREFERRED COLOUR SCHEME

WARDROBE COLOUR SCHEME

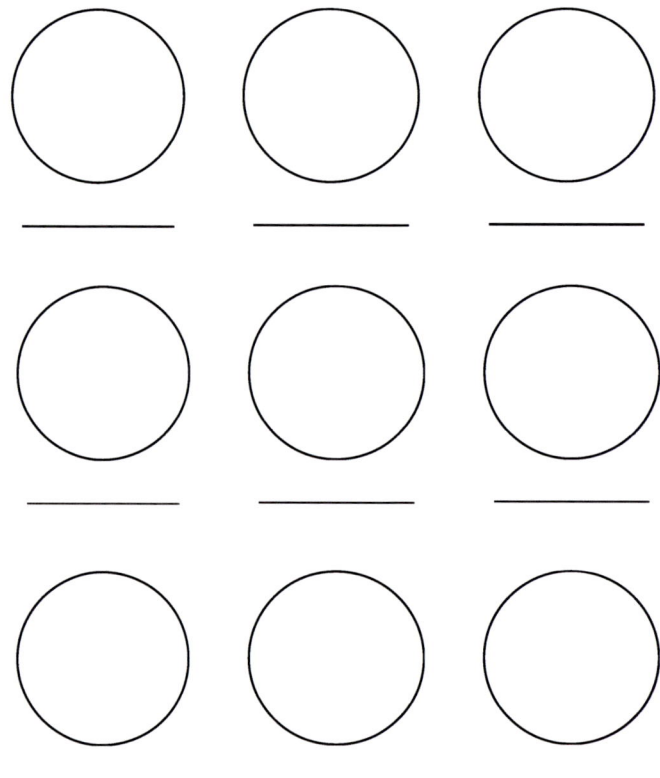

WARDROBE CLEANSE RITUAL

MODULE 4

FAVOURITE COLOURS

When adding new items to your wardrobe, draw inspiration from your favourite coloUrs

WARDROBE CLEANSE RITUAL

MODULE 4

WRITE DOWN WHAT YOU'VE LEARNED IN THIS MODULE, INCLUDING ALL THE KEY POINTS.

WARDROBE CLEANSE RITUAL

MODULE 4

By completing the Wardrobe Cleanse Ritual Module, you have gained valuable knowledge and skills to create a functional wardrobe that genuinely represents your unique style.

A curated wardrobe empowers us and helps us connect with our authenticity.

MODULE 5

NEW STYLE COMBINATIONS

RECAPTURE YOUR STYLE ESSENCE BY BRINGING TOGETHER INSPIRING COMBINATIONS

Try New Style Combinations And Document Your Journey.

MODULE 5

PLAY YOUR FAVOURITE TUNES AND GET YOUR STYLE RUNWAY READY.

Take full-length photographs of your favourite combinations that work with your lifestyle.

Have a friend take pictures or set a self-timer on your camera.

Keep the photographs ready and available when you need to recapture your unique style essence.

NEW STYLE COMBINATIONS

MODULE 5

USE THE FOLLOWING PAGES IN THIS MODULE TO TAKE NOTES OF YOUR OUTFIT COMBINATIONS.

Note if an outfit suits a particular occasion or special event or helps you feel confident.

STEP 1: OUTFIT INSPIRATION
Discover new style ideas and capture them in your notes

STEP 2: STYLE PLANNER
Experiment with different styles and outfits using clothes you own and document your journey

STEP 3: FAVOURITE ITEMS
Note down your favourite clothing pieces, including their colour and how you can mix and match them with other items

NEW STYLE COMBINATIONS

MODULE 5

OUTFIT INSPIRATION

STYLE:

_____

_____

_____

SEASON/WEATHER:

_____

_____

_____

OCCASION:

_____

_____

_____

NOTES:

_____

_____

_____

NEW STYLE COMBINATIONS

MODULE 5

OUTFIT INSPIRATION

STYLE:

_____

_____

_____

_____

SEASON/WEATHER:

_____

_____

_____

OCCASION:

_____

_____

_____

NOTES:

_____

_____

_____

NEW STYLE COMBINATIONS

MODULE 5

OUTFIT INSPIRATION

STYLE:

_____

_____

_____

SEASON/WEATHER:

_____

_____

OCCASION:

_____

_____

_____

NOTES:

_____

_____

_____

NEW STYLE COMBINATIONS

MODULE 5

OUTFIT INSPIRATION

STYLE:

_____

_____

_____

SEASON/WEATHER:

_____

_____

_____

OCCASION:

_____

_____

_____

NOTES:

_____

_____

_____

NEW STYLE COMBINATIONS

MODULE 5

OUTFIT INSPIRATION

STYLE:

_____

_____

_____

_____

SEASON/WEATHER:

_____

_____

_____

OCCASION:

_____

_____

_____

NOTES:

_____

_____

_____

NEW STYLE COMBINATIONS

MODULE 5

OUTFIT INSPIRATION

STYLE:

_____

_____

_____

_____

SEASON/WEATHER:

_____

_____

_____

OCCASION:

_____

_____

_____

NOTES:

_____

_____

_____

_____

NEW STYLE COMBINATIONS

MODULE 5

OUTFIT INSPIRATION

STYLE:

_____

_____

_____

_____

SEASON/WEATHER:

_____

_____

_____

OCCASION:

_____

_____

_____

NOTES:

_____

_____

_____

NEW STYLE COMBINATIONS

MODULE 5

OUTFIT INSPIRATION

STYLE:

_____

_____

_____

SEASON/WEATHER:

_____

_____

_____

OCCASION:

_____

_____

_____

NOTES:

_____

_____

_____

NEW STYLE COMBINATIONS

MODULE 5

STYLE PLANNER

WEATHER _____

OCCASSION _____

TOPS _____

BOTTOMS _____

SHOES _____

ACCESSORIES _____

LAYERS/EXTRAS _____

STYLE-CHECK IN

HOW DO YOU FEEL WEARING THIS OUTFIT?

_____

_____

_____

MONTHLY OUTFIT CHECK-IN

_____

_____

_____

WOULD YOU LIKE TO MAKE ANY ADDITIONS OR ALTERATIONS TO THIS OUTFIT?

_____

_____

_____

OUTFIT:

◯ ◯ ◯ ◯ ◯

COLOUR PALETTE

NEW STYLE COMBINATIONS

MODULE 5

STYLE PLANNER

WEATHER _____

OCCASSION _____

TOPS _____

BOTTOMS _____

SHOES _____

ACCESSORIES _____

LAYERS/EXTRAS _____

STYLE-CHECK IN

HOW DO YOU FEEL WEARING THIS OUTFIT?

_____

_____

_____

MONTHLY OUTFIT CHECK-IN

_____

_____

_____

WOULD YOU LIKE TO MAKE ANY ADDITIONS OR ALTERATIONS TO THIS OUTFIT?

_____

_____

_____

OUTFIT:

◯ ◯ ◯ ◯ ◯

COLOUR PALETTE

NEW STYLE COMBINATIONS

MODULE 5

STYLE PLANNER

WEATHER _____

OCCASSION _____

TOPS _____

BOTTOMS _____

SHOES _____

ACCESSORIES _____

LAYERS/EXTRAS _____

STYLE-CHECK IN

HOW DO YOU FEEL WEARING THIS OUTFIT?

_____

_____

_____

MONTHLY OUTFIT CHECK-IN

_____

_____

_____

WOULD YOU LIKE TO MAKE ANY ADDITIONS OR ALTERATIONS TO THIS OUTFIT?

_____

_____

_____

OUTFIT:

◯ ◯ ◯ ◯ ◯

COLOUR PALETTE

NEW STYLE COMBINATIONS

MODULE 5

STYLE PLANNER

WEATHER _____

OCCASSION _____

TOPS _____

BOTTOMS _____

SHOES _____

ACCESSORIES _____

LAYERS/EXTRAS _____

STYLE-CHECK IN

HOW DO YOU FEEL WEARING THIS OUTFIT?

_____

_____

_____

MONTHLY OUTFIT CHECK-IN

_____

_____

_____

WOULD YOU LIKE TO MAKE ANY ADDITIONS OR ALTERATIONS TO THIS OUTFIT?

_____

_____

_____

OUTFIT:

○ ○ ○ ○ ○

COLOUR PALETTE

NEW STYLE COMBINATIONS

MODULE 5

STYLE PLANNER

WEATHER _____

OCCASSION _____

TOPS _____

BOTTOMS _____

SHOES _____

ACCESSORIES _____

LAYERS/EXTRAS _____

STYLE-CHECK IN

HOW DO YOU FEEL WEARING THIS OUTFIT?

_____

_____

_____

MONTHLY OUTFIT CHECK-IN

_____

_____

_____

WOULD YOU LIKE TO MAKE ANY ADDITIONS OR ALTERATIONS TO THIS OUTFIT?

_____

_____

_____

OUTFIT:

◯ ◯ ◯ ◯ ◯

COLOUR PALETTE

NEW STYLE COMBINATIONS

MODULE 5

STYLE PLANNER

WEATHER _____

OCCASSION _____

TOPS _____

BOTTOMS _____

SHOES _____

ACCESSORIES _____

LAYERS/EXTRAS _____

STYLE-CHECK IN

HOW DO YOU FEEL WEARING THIS OUTFIT?

_____

_____

_____

MONTHLY OUTFIT CHECK-IN

_____

_____

_____

WOULD YOU LIKE TO MAKE ANY ADDITIONS OR ALTERATIONS TO THIS OUTFIT?

_____

_____

_____

OUTFIT:

○ ○ ○ ○ ○

COLOUR PALETTE

NEW STYLE COMBINATIONS

MODULE 5

STYLE PLANNER

WEATHER _____

OCCASSION _____

TOPS _____

BOTTOMS _____

SHOES _____

ACCESSORIES _____

LAYERS/EXTRAS _____

STYLE-CHECK IN

HOW DO YOU FEEL WEARING THIS OUTFIT?

_____

_____

_____

MONTHLY OUTFIT CHECK-IN

_____

_____

_____

WOULD YOU LIKE TO MAKE ANY ADDITIONS OR ALTERATIONS TO THIS OUTFIT?

_____

_____

_____

OUTFIT:

◯ ◯ ◯ ◯ ◯

COLOUR PALETTE

NEW STYLE COMBINATIONS

MODULE 5

STYLE PLANNER

WEATHER _____

OCCASSION _____

TOPS _____

BOTTOMS _____

SHOES _____

ACCESSORIES _____

LAYERS/EXTRAS _____

STYLE-CHECK IN

HOW DO YOU FEEL WEARING THIS OUTFIT?

_____

_____

_____

MONTHLY OUTFIT CHECK-IN

_____

_____

_____

WOULD YOU LIKE TO MAKE ANY ADDITIONS OR ALTERATIONS TO THIS OUTFIT?

_____

_____

_____

OUTFIT:

◯ ◯ ◯ ◯ ◯

COLOUR PALETTE

NEW STYLE COMBINATIONS

MODULE 5

STYLE PLANNER

WEATHER _____

OCCASSION _____

TOPS _____

BOTTOMS _____

SHOES _____

ACCESSORIES _____

LAYERS/EXTRAS _____

STYLE-CHECK IN

HOW DO YOU FEEL WEARING THIS OUTFIT?

MONTHLY OUTFIT CHECK-IN

WOULD YOU LIKE TO MAKE ANY ADDITIONS OR ALTERATIONS TO THIS OUTFIT?

OUTFIT:

○ ○ ○ ○ ○

COLOUR PALETTE

NEW STYLE COMBINATIONS

MODULE 5

FAVOURITE CLOTHING ITEMS

STYLE

COLOUR PALETTE

WHEN WEARING THIS CLOTHING ITEM, PAY ATTENTION TO HOW IT FEELS AND HOW IT CAN BE COMBINED WITH OTHER PIECES IN YOUR WARDROBE.

NEW STYLE COMBINATIONS

MODULE 5

FAVOURITE CLOTHING ITEMS

STYLE

COLOUR PALETTE

WHEN WEARING THIS CLOTHING ITEM, PAY ATTENTION TO HOW IT FEELS AND HOW IT CAN BE COMBINED WITH OTHER PIECES IN YOUR WARDROBE.

NEW STYLE COMBINATIONS

MODULE 5

FAVOURITE CLOTHING ITEMS

STYLE

COLOUR PALETTE

WHEN WEARING THIS CLOTHING ITEM, PAY ATTENTION TO HOW IT FEELS AND HOW IT CAN BE COMBINED WITH OTHER PIECES IN YOUR WARDROBE.

NEW STYLE COMBINATIONS

MODULE 5

FAVOURITE CLOTHING ITEMS

STYLE

COLOUR PALETTE

WHEN WEARING THIS CLOTHING ITEM, PAY ATTENTION TO HOW IT FEELS AND HOW IT CAN BE COMBINED WITH OTHER PIECES IN YOUR WARDROBE.

NEW STYLE COMBINATIONS

MODULE 5

FAVOURITE CLOTHING ITEMS

STYLE

COLOUR PALETTE

WHEN WEARING THIS CLOTHING ITEM, PAY ATTENTION TO HOW IT FEELS
AND HOW IT CAN BE COMBINED WITH OTHER PIECES IN YOUR WARDROBE.

NEW STYLE COMBINATIONS

MODULE 5

FAVOURITE CLOTHING ITEMS

STYLE

COLOUR PALETTE

WHEN WEARING THIS CLOTHING ITEM, PAY ATTENTION TO HOW IT FEELS AND HOW IT CAN BE COMBINED WITH OTHER PIECES IN YOUR WARDROBE.

NEW STYLE COMBINATIONS

MODULE 5

FAVOURITE CLOTHING ITEMS

STYLE

COLOUR PALETTE

WHEN WEARING THIS CLOTHING ITEM, PAY ATTENTION TO HOW IT FEELS AND HOW IT CAN BE COMBINED WITH OTHER PIECES IN YOUR WARDROBE.

NEW STYLE COMBINATIONS

MODULE 5

FAVOURITE CLOTHING ITEMS

STYLE

COLOUR PALETTE

WHEN WEARING THIS CLOTHING ITEM, PAY ATTENTION TO HOW IT FEELS AND HOW IT CAN BE COMBINED WITH OTHER PIECES IN YOUR WARDROBE.

NEW STYLE COMBINATIONS

MODULE 5

FAVOURITE CLOTHING ITEMS

STYLE

COLOUR PALETTE

WHEN WEARING THIS CLOTHING ITEM, PAY ATTENTION TO HOW IT FEELS
AND HOW IT CAN BE COMBINED WITH OTHER PIECES IN YOUR WARDROBE.

NEW STYLE COMBINATIONS

MODULE 5

FAVOURITE CLOTHING ITEMS

STYLE

COLOUR PALETTE

WHEN WEARING THIS CLOTHING ITEM, PAY ATTENTION TO HOW IT FEELS
AND HOW IT CAN BE COMBINED WITH OTHER PIECES IN YOUR WARDROBE.

NEW STYLE COMBINATIONS

MODULE 5

WHAT HAVE YOU LEARNED IN THIS MODULE?

NEW STYLE COMBINATIONS

MODULE 5

This module helps us explore our style choices, allowing us to authentically express ourselves and discover new ways to showcase our individuality through clothing.

CONGRATULATIONS

your wardrobe cleanse is complete!

CONGRATULATIONS
ON TAKING THE FIRST
STEPS TOWARDS
EXPLORING YOUR
STYLE AND
WARDROBE

Regularly performing a wardrobe cleanse ritual can enhance self-confidence and develop a healthy relationship with your clothing and style choices.

Remember to stay consistent with your style foundations, always keep learning, and be prepared to experience the magic of a well-curated wardrobe!

YOU HAVE
COMPLETED
YOUR INTUITIVE
WARDROBE
CLEANSE

Intuitive Style x

Turn the page to discover the Style Notebook section. It's designed to help you reflect on and evolve your unique style through any changes.

STYLE NOTEBBOOK

STYLE NOTEBOOK

TAKE A MOMENT TO REFLECT ON YOUR STYLE JOURNEY AND ITS POSITIVE IMPACT ON YOUR CREATIVITY AND CONFIDENCE

Keeping a style journal, creating mood boards, making lists, and developing your unique style over time will help you keep motivated and inspired on your style journey

STYLE NOTEBOOK

REFLECTING ON YOUR JOURNEY OF CLEANSING YOUR WARDROBE...
HOW DO YOU FEEL? HAVE THERE BEEN ANY POSITIVE IMPACTS?

STYLE NOTEBOOK

HAVE YOU NOTICED ANY SIGNIFICANT CHANGES IN YOURSELF AND YOUR STYLE?

STYLE NOTEBOOK

DURING YOUR WARDROBE CLEANSE JOURNEY, WHAT WERE THE THINGS THAT STOOD OUT TO YOU THE MOST?

STYLE NOTEBOOK

DO YOU HAVE ANY IDEAS FOR A FUTURE WARDROBE REVAMP?

STYLE NOTEBOOK

UNLEASH YOUR CREATIVITY AND GATHER WARDROBE INSPIRATION IN THIS SPACE

WARDROBE
MOOD BOARD

DRAW INSPIRATION AND EXPLORE STYLE IDEAS IN THIS SPACE

STYLE MOOD BOARD

STYLE JOURNAL

Come back to this journaling space anytime you want to explore your unique style further.

DATE:

STYLE JOURNAL

DATE:

STYLE JOURNAL

DATE:

STYLE JOURNAL

DATE:

STYLE JOURNAL

DATE:

STYLE JOURNAL

DATE:

STYLE JOURNAL

DATE:

STYLE JOURNAL

DATE:

STYLE JOURNAL

DATE:

STYLE JOURNAL

DATE:

STYLE JOURNAL

DATE:

STYLE JOURNAL

DATE:

STYLE JOURNAL

DATE:

STYLE JOURNAL

DATE:

STYLE JOURNAL

DATE:

STYLE JOURNAL

DATE:

STYLE JOURNAL

DATE:

STYLE JOURNAL

DATE:

STYLE LISTS

- [ ] _____
- [ ] _____
- [ ] _____
- [ ] _____
- [ ] _____
- [ ] _____
- [ ] _____
- [ ] _____
- [ ] _____

The style list pages can be used for various purposes, such as updating your wardrobe, planning travel outfits, creating wishlists, and more.

STYLE LISTS

- ☐ _____
- ☐ _____
- ☐ _____
- ☐ _____
- ☐ _____
- ☐ _____
- ☐ _____
- ☐ _____
- ☐ _____
- ☐ _____

STYLE LISTS

☐ _____

☐ _____

☐ _____

☐ _____

☐ _____

☐ _____

☐ _____

☐ _____

☐ _____

☐ _____

STYLE LISTS

- ☐ _____
- ☐ _____
- ☐ _____
- ☐ _____
- ☐ _____
- ☐ _____
- ☐ _____
- ☐ _____
- ☐ _____
- ☐ _____

STYLE LISTS

- [ ] _____
- [ ] _____
- [ ] _____
- [ ] _____
- [ ] _____
- [ ] _____
- [ ] _____
- [ ] _____
- [ ] _____
- [ ] _____

STYLE LISTS

- ☐
- ☐
- ☐
- ☐
- ☐
- ☐
- ☐
- ☐
- ☐
- ☐

STYLE LISTS

- ☐ _____
- ☐ _____
- ☐ _____
- ☐ _____
- ☐ _____
- ☐ _____
- ☐ _____
- ☐ _____
- ☐ _____
- ☐ _____

STYLE LISTS

- [ ]
- [ ]
- [ ]
- [ ]
- [ ]
- [ ]
- [ ]
- [ ]
- [ ]
- [ ]

STYLE LISTS

- ☐ _____
- ☐ _____
- ☐ _____
- ☐ _____
- ☐ _____
- ☐ _____
- ☐ _____
- ☐ _____
- ☐ _____
- ☐ _____

STYLE LISTS

- [ ] _____
- [ ] _____
- [ ] _____
- [ ] _____
- [ ] _____
- [ ] _____
- [ ] _____
- [ ] _____
- [ ] _____
- [ ] _____

STYLE LISTS

- [ ] _____
- [ ] _____
- [ ] _____
- [ ] _____
- [ ] _____
- [ ] _____
- [ ] _____
- [ ] _____
- [ ] _____
- [ ] _____

STYLE LISTS

- [ ] _____
- [ ] _____
- [ ] _____
- [ ] _____
- [ ] _____
- [ ] _____
- [ ] _____
- [ ] _____
- [ ] _____
- [ ] _____

Undertaking a Wardrobe Cleanse Ritual can be a powerful and transformative experience that allows us to discover more about ourselves.

By practising self-love and self-care, we can create space for new energy to flow into our lives and fill our soul, body and mind with love.

Through this process, we can gain clarity and insight into what makes us feel good and establish a deeper connection with our unique selves.

EXPRESSING GRATITUDE FOR YOUR SELF-INVESTMENT AND ONGOING SUPPORT

THE INTUITIVE WARDROBE CLEANSE FORMULA:
WORKBOOK & GUIDE.

By Chandra Lucinda founder of Intuitive Style

IMAGE CONSULTANT /STYLIST
& CONTENT CREATOR IN AUSTRALIA

KEEP IN TOUCH

INTUITIVE STYLE

style & self-love rituals

WWW.INTUITIVESTYLE.CO

COPYRIGHT

COPYRIGHT © 2023 BY INTUITIVE STYLE
ALL RIGHTS RESERVED

www.ingramcontent.com/pod-product-compliance
Lightning Source LLC
Chambersburg PA
CBRC092341290426
44109CB00009B/179